SCATTERED

poems by

Kenneth Francis Pearson

SCARMORA PRESS

for Cory Lynn

"I love you in this life and all our lives to come."

SCATTERED

Send all inquiries to the following address:

Scarmora Press
236 E. Mountain Alder Street
Sahuarita, AZ 85629

First Edition
Printed in the United States of America
ISBN: 978-0-9768543-0-2

Cover & Interior Design:
Kenneth Francis Pearson

OTHER BOOKS BY KENNETH FRANCIS PEARSON

The Old Leather Room
(Cyberwit, 2004)

Water Falls In Autumn: Verse vs. Adversity
(Amarcord Press, 2007)

PREVIOUSLY PUBLISHED POEMS

- "SHADOW OF THE MAPLE TREE" was the winner of the 2017 Greater New York State Fair's Poetry Competition

- "GONE THE WAY" is an alternate version of the poem "I" which was previously published in the 2004 release THE OLD LEATHER ROOM

- "EXCEPT TO YOU" and "OUR GOODBYES" first appeared in the Winter 2020 issue of the Remington Review

- "BEFORE DAWN" first appeared in the Winter 2020 issue of The Night Heron Barks

TABLE OF CONTENTS

I.

*"Self-reflection is necessary to dig beneath our own layers
and visit the inner crevices of our heart and mind
to develop an understanding of life."*
– Unknown

SHADOW OF THE MAPLE TREE

He has been stripped to the barest of skeletons – bones bared
like the frozen, dark branches of the winter maple tree.

He stands humbled and ethereal, above the frosted tips of wild grass,
as each blade is beckoned skyward, through a plaid of faded memories.

He has prepared for the long, icy slumber, and dreams ebulliently
of his shadow as it covers the scattered leaves upon the valley floor.

He listens silently as the symphony of winter embarks on its finale –
and rollicks in whispered contentment for a springtime soon to come.

His balanced wisdom nourishes earth's blackened soil – and gives promise
for a vibrant resurrection in the grandest of spring awakenings.

MIND. BODY. SOUL.

Writing is not about glory, nor fame,
it is not about personal reward.

It is the stamp at the end of the sentence,
a signature, a last word.

It is an emphasis on the syllable,
or the liquidity of language,

being pulled from the burning building,
while life hinders in the balance.

It is late nights, and early mornings.
It is missed birthdays.

It is forgotten memories.
It is memories never existing.

It is an intense glimpse at the world
through an overstimulated lens.

It is an internal struggle,
a weed grasping at your soul.

It is the constant argument,
between the rational and irrational,

between brain and heart,
between life and death.

It questions meaning,
and dances with colors.

It is the first breath taken,
and the last breath stolen.

It is everything and nothing.
It teeters on madness.

It is being surrounded by the world,
but alone in your head.

It is the fear of success,
and the acceptance of failure.

It is a passion which extinguishes your flame,
and leaves you dying amongst the embers of infinity.

Writing is the solo exhibition, the exploration
of the deepest of caverns.

It is Mind.
 It is Body.
  It is Soul.

SLUMBER OF MOUNTAINS

Undisturbed is the slumber of mountains,
like the absence of childhood memories,
impelled from the caverns of mind.

The vision of their world cascades toward constellations,
and through the ambivalence of anchored trees,
amicable and entrenched in the obdurate earth.

Disharmonious to the mind of the nomad,
the molesters of silentious meditation,
illimitable itinerants who have displaced the disinherited.

The heart of the asperous mountains endures
an amaranthine admiration, and know existence no other,
then the pacific permanence of solitude.

SPACE-TIME CONTINUUM

I cannot remember what it is like to be young –
to run carelessly on dirt paths,
which led into the caves of my memory.

I cannot remember what it is like to wonder –
about the world's dizzying rotation,
while I watch the spin of the merry-go-round.

I cannot remember what it is like to wander -
a child's innocence like the freedom of a comet
that shoots through the vastness of the –

Space-Time Continuum.

I remember this morning –
awoken to the weight of Atlas' world on my chest,
a gasp, a cough, then the tremors of nerves.

I remember this morning –
the face in the mirror like Tintern Abbey,
two centuries removed.

I remember this morning –
and the translucency of emotional withdrawal,
but I cannot remember how this morning came to be.

HIBERNATION OF THE SUBCONSCIOUS MIND

On a roadless travel, we wander,
with trees crackling,
in a summer, thunderstorm wind.

Aimless and guide-less,
we discover broken clouds
and the hint of autumn, as it breathes
through the smell of petrichor.
For a single moment,
there is no drenching humidity
or motion halting heat.

Gusts,
  leaves,
    thunder,
    lightning breaks the sky in two.

We wander on a muddy, murky path,
to a home with distant and forgotten memories.

I have changed, not you.
I now see who you are, even
if I was blinded by myself.

A weight gone.
A new weight added.

Home,
  I do not recognize you.

My voice, one of inquisitive anxiousness.
  Hers, a sound of monotonous death.

Where have you been?
  I've been trapped within myself.

The world is ugly now.
  The world has been ugly, always.

How has your life been all these years?
> *Challenging.*

Why?
> *Perceptions through a broken telescope.*

Where are you going?
> *I am leaving so I may go back within myself.*

What are you going to do?
> *Think.*

About what?
> *Life.*

Shall I see you soon?
> *In another lifetime.*

But, why so long?
> *Thought is an arduous chore.*

Your thought will take a lifetime?
> *It took me a lifetime to get here.*

But haven't you always lived here?
> *Only physically.*

But aren't you alive?
> *Only physically.*

What will you do?
> *Hibernate.*

Sleep?
> *It is a Hibernation of the Subconscious Mind.*

But will you be awake?
> *Only physically.*

Will I be able to speak with you?
Requests will go unanswered.

I don't understand.
There is nothing to understand.

What shall I do in the meantime?
Live.

But how can I live without thought?
There are many others that have been successful before you.

But ... but ... I prefer thinking.
Do you?

(Pause) I believe so.
Your hesitation creates uncertainty.

I am not uncertain.
Ah, my dearest friend.
Good is the night,
but darkness always reigns before dawn.
We stare up in silence.
Whispers call back from the stars.
A crescent moon. A shimmer.
A mind forgiven. A life forgotten.
These are the enemies we now call friends.
These are the times of chaotic embrace.
Our final undoing in the grand scheme
of ever-aloneness.

DAY SILENCE

the days are quiet –

they are a silence which sits
like a clay face burned from wind.

they envelop fragility,
and cover the head with a black sack.

they pull oxygen from the air
and gasp! suffocate the soul.

dreams die in a soundless void,
and silence becomes the gut-rot of a failed poet.

silence is the guillotine severed hand,
the swinging of Poe's pendulum,

the masquerade, the façade,
the uninspired smile.

silence is the torture of a hostile mind,
the embraced madness,

interrupted by corruption,
and the yearn for impact.

YOU LEFT TOO SOON

In the early morning, I rise. Yawn. And
listen to your saved telephone message,
        your voice echoing in the background wind.

I open a bottle of water I take from the refrigerator
        and gulp down pills that help me forget.

I look out the window. There is still no sign of day.

I open the door, see the brightness of the stars,
        and my thoughts turn to you.

                You left too soon.

I pack a cigarette,
        the flicker of sparks,
                and connect the dots in the sky.

                You left too soon.

The fragrance of your hair remains trapped,
        in a sweatshirt you left behind.

A raccoon stares indifferent.
        The crackle of a tobacco song, sung   .
                by wasted oxygen pulled from the air,
                        smoke billows, one breath closer to death.

Sleepy clouds blanket the sky,
        and extinguish burning diamonds.
        Thoughts, like you, vanish.

The glow from the city rises,
        miles away where your glow resides.

                You left too soon.

Yours was a tender smile.
> The breeze bellows and beckons
>> the branches of the trees,
>>> the whisper of leaves,
>> and your soft lips against my ear.

> You left too soon.

There were ten-thousand souls
> who stirred in the echo of your eyes,
>> but you were only a fraction of your former self.

Faded is my mirrored reflection.

All has been a stagnant black hole
> since you've been gone.
>> And I blame you because you…

> You left too soon.

GONE THE WAY

i've seen the mirrored lives,
from ancient distant skies,
stare back into my rainbow eyes.

echoed are the painful cries
of a thousand souls' winded sighs,
disappointed by neglected ties.

faded is a primitive lullaby,
gone the way of the river quay,
with me, this heritage shall die.

i am my lie.
i am my lie.
i am i.

HERE

Here, the dark sky blankets the quiet man,
as he gazes upon the stars,
through thicket and leaves.

Here, he carves his legacy,
into a cosmic constellation.

Here, his mind is boundless,
free to reconcile the individual
who practices making shadow puppets
in the daylight hours.

Here, he is alone with his new friend – thought –
and a new moon fades into the blackness of the night sky.

Here, his may be a blank existence,
but he has been liberated from the confines imposed
by an unfulfilled life.

II.

*"At night I closed my eyes and saw my bones
threading the mud of my grave."*
- Jack Kerouac

3:00 am

warehouse graveyard shifts are for cold, decadent eyes who stare ahead at
solid walls. individuals deafened by the hum of a conveyor, and the
concrete foot trample which sings of blue-collar existence.

all is well in the smoker's section at 3:00 am, where people fill their lungs with
enough poison to tighten the gap between living and dying. an uninspired
artist describes the process of art, as she fidgets with her bag,

her armpits exposed with hair longer than mine. she never believed she had
talent, but perhaps she only needed encouragement, which an older man gives,
even though he's never picked up a brush,

except when he painted his daughter's room, when she was young, before she
and his wife decided they were better off without him.

he tells the story then falls silent, while an older woman who sits nearby,
a woman whom he has befriended, glances at him with the eyes of a lover,
concern worn like a canvass on her face, but notice he doesn't, as he looks

off in the distance to an empty dark night, with a black backdrop
as his only reprieve to a life filled with regrets. he lights a cigarette and
takes a deep inhalation, then exhales the remainder of his soul,

while the demons of his past beat upon his chest. there is purpose
in his actions, purpose in the smoke which billows from the shell.

warehouses are prisons filled with regrets, filled with the remainders of
society's lamented, filled with the lost and barely surviving. they embrace the
destitute, while the rest of the world sleeps in the comfort of their dreams,

and those barely conscious, call home.

GROUNDSKEEPER AT A CEMETERY

In the rickety old shack, the oak planks murmur in whispered echoes,
as he shuffles across the hallway and through the front door.

His life has become a stagnation of time,
filled with the malodor of stale cigarettes and mold.

Outside, the fog bellows below the mourning stars
and moans through a finite dusky grey.

He methodically walks the secluded foot worn path,
to avoid the shadows cast by the glow of the moon's wane.

He inhales the silver mist at the gate of the old cemetery,
as the sky respires the last of the morning dew.

He wipes the wrought-iron post and polishes the center of the weight-sagged
double gate, with the outer sleeve of his shirt,

And speaks to his companions beneath the moss-covered gravestones,
as he stares torpidly at their disillusioned epitaphs.

He has been honored by life's sole privilege – longevity,
with ample ability to saunter silently down the inscripted alley.

He, the declared Master of Ceremony in Death's parade.

*

He lifts his shovel and plunges it into the earth.
The dirt embraces his lugubrious advance.

If this be a tedious preparation for the afterlife, he thinks,
I am the requisite, for man must dig man's own grave.

When the procession arrives, he shall stand at a distance,
to not disturb the grief-stricken cavalcade of black-adorned mourners.

He shall wait to cover the oak coffin with dirt,
until the earth's porous soil reclaims the last of the living tears.

Pleading prayers howled toward the heavens, then vanish
like white noise in the storm of deafened ears.

His shall be the final touch felt, the final rose placed.
His shall be the final teardrop fallen, the final words spoken,

Long before the memories begin to fade,
in the minds of those left sorrowful and dying.

His feet will root like the newly planted seeds,
above the new home of his silent companion,

And each day, he will delight in the epitaphs of the dead,
as he saunters silently down the inscripted alley.

His oath – to inhibit the neglect of the lamented,
until no longer can he execute his Master of Ceremony – In this,

the solitary commemoration of life's departed.

WANDERER

You are the golden sun,
born of sound mind,
and the chaotic masterpiece
of a pre-destined future.

Greatness is determined by the presence
of the wandering jungle man –
        as he sings in silence,
        as he smiles in sadness,
        as he gazes at gateways.

It is he who shares his eyes.

STRANDED

a smooth, rounded rock lies in the white sand
on a deserted shore. her sorrow drowns at high tide.
at low, she is stranded alone to
contemplate the vastness of the ocean and the
insignificance of her life. her sorrow grows, as
she is taught no different. she just stares over
the horizon, anchored in the sand, searching
for a sign of the man she used to love.

UNSETTLED

laborious truth untold,
mirror's mocked soul
and stole…

…in,

a preacher's sermon,
a prophesized demon.

questions impose
words written prose
and eyes' glow…

…in,

hell, she walks,
her choices, her faults.

a secret's silent confusion.

STALKING PREY

'tis consciousness that corrupts my mind,
i feel no remorse for my being.

there is sadness in her touch. a cold grasp of
the piercing of ice destined to wither into obscurity.

one moment, she sings her glory. the next,
she is stalking prey.

SOMETIMES

Sometimes,
loneliness is overwhelming,
and sadness rings
through the blackened
darkness of night.

Sometimes,
all I wish,
is to be vulnerable,
and not be forced to sleep
within the falsity of hope.

SIMPLICITY

All life can be found,
in the simplicity of a genuine smile.

VAGABOND

When we live,
the sunlight seems to dance,
through a broken tree branch,
and we can find on our face,
the warmth of a smile.

... AND LAUGHTER

Her curious blue eyes,
>   stare at the world in which she lives,
>   unaware of the struggles of her parents,
>   unaware of the state of the world.

She knows only,
>   the rip of paper and laughter,
>   the scream at cats and laughter,
>   the crawl to couch and laughter.

She knows only,
>   bottled milk and mashed rice,
>   confines and playpens,
>   the loving gaze of eyes.

The simplicity of experience is not wasted on her.

It is her existence.

MAYFLY

He forgets to breathe, sometimes,
as he sits motionless on the corner rocking chair.
He stares blankly at an empty television screen,
and recites a poem learned long ago.

He lives like the mayfly as it dances above a rounded stone,
and dives to touch the water as it ripples along the shore.
He is isolated by the mountain stream, secluded by summer trees;
his eyes gleam and reflect the rays of the sun.

He talks of mountain summer storms and turbulent winds,
the rain which trickled through maple leaves and he,
with wings damp and grounded, cried at the sight of a starry night,
before being silently covered by a blanket of earth.

He closes his eyes and fades into a lover's dream; he worries not
for what his sleep entails – his existence is beyond love's decay.
With night's final breath, his memory will die, to be reborn in the morning,
without recollection of the day he lived as a mayfly.

III.

"I know the ones who love us will miss us."
- Keanu Reeves

BEFORE DAWN

in a pacific twilight,
before the sun ascends the eastern mountains,
before the world blossoms from luminous grey,
and dew transforms into nullity,

there is a silent background,
before the restlessness of the world awakens,
and heard is the clarity of the morning song,
sung by a voice of heaven.

as the air lies quiet in heart's stillness,
and a single teardrop caresses the empty sky,
ours are the onliest eyes alighted,
upon the boon of the springing dawn.

you reach to me your hand, and in my palm,
a line is drawn with the tip of your finger.
sent is a synapse of harmonious connection,
which comes to rest in our solitary existence.

THE SOFT WHISPER OF AN ARCTIC BREEZE

in the frozen tundra she sings,
against the soft whisper of an arctic breeze.

her hand touches his, and revives
the soul of a man who died long ago.

frozen blood melts, then pulsates through his veins,
pumping life into the fallen snow.

she has finally returned, he thinks,
the angel who had forgotten him years ago.

forgotten, against all memory,
the harshness of his existence.

she who traveled toward an unattainable hope,
while he remained stagnant in his own dysphoria.

it is the piercing of her eyes he fears,
for he has never been the one to accept forgiveness.

but neither has she,
ever learned to forgive.

STILL REAL

I.

It is her eyes which drive me – seafoam green pulchritudinous
shadows glimpse into heaven's soul.

Her face triangular, linear, round, accentuating each simple curve with light
skin and a quiver in her smile – her voice soothes and calms me – always
calms me.

She breaks into song as she strums an air guitar and feels
comfort from me. I wish I could kiss her lips. It is today, and she is still real
and I am still real.

That is all I can ask.

II.

I have seen inside the gates of heaven, floating quietly on a cloud, with my
soul becoming inflamed with infatuation and love.

You wonder if I know the consequences of my actions. I gift a beautifully trag-
ic life, inviting heartache and confusion.

I wish for you to smile, though, to see that life does not have to dwell in a rot-
ting pool. Beautiful sorrow, we all must live, for I would rather die alone with
my words then settle for anything less than my expectations.

III.

A soul search,
a time for the rustle of torn stars which dwell in the possibilities
of what could have been.

An indiscretion,
for the mending heart is brought to me to be fixed – but why
must my heart be the one to break?

Words are filtered into my ears,
and contradicted with actions.
Who am I to play the fool?

MOURNING BIRD

stern mourning   bird in song
sings sadness   and yearns for love
       ingested by her tender heart

hers   the saddened existence
with broken   wing
      still to mend

it flutters   in absence
of air   which resonates
      through sunlight

i call   to her
in a soft   sultry voice
     but she does not answer

and still   is the mourn
with a gentle breeze   the leaves prance
      upon the trees

and still   she sings
her mourning song   to hollow air
     it goes answered

but listen   i do
and sing   she does
     in the earliest of mourning

yet, never   does it waver
though   her love
     will never come

but sing   she does
and to me   my heart
     heeds the call

ORCHID IN LATE MAY

Her vitriol is a diamond rubbed on glass,
a crop circle carved in the mouths of famine.

My vitriol is the callousness of emotions,
a silent infant swaddled in a dumpster.

Together we are an unwritten exposition,
a song sung into the deafness of ears.

We are the pulse on the floor,
an unpublicized disaster.

We are the grotesque love of movies,
the bitterness of cucurbitacin.

She is an orchid in late May,
and I, I am the rose in December.

GARDEN IN A CITY

on a manicured path,
we walk through fallen cotton balls

in an inverted pollen-soaked bowl,
like snow, souls dance in a windless theatre.

hers is the heart which pokes through sand,
mine are the feet which sink in the wetland.

it is a lost valley among a city,
a city which disturbs the well -

lit light of a cloudless sky
in an afternoon that basks in isolation.

alone, with her, with me, accompanied
by a swarm of hungry mosquitos.

we feast on love,
they feast on us.

WHAT SAY THEE THEN?

What say thee then?

When ears deafen
    to the gurgled gasp
        of a drowned man.

When crooked smiles
    and distant eyes
        cry behind drawn curtains.

When a masquerade ball's
    masks are revealed
        to be a faceless one.

When fingers touch letters,
    letters touch eyes,
        eyes shun minds.

What say thee then?

IF ONLY

She stretches her arms to the harvest moon,
and with her fingers, touches the air
which leads to the night sky pinnacle.

I am the nightingale, she proclaims.

The stars glitter in the reflection of her eyes.

This is a frozen moment of undeterred significance.

I cannot be drawn to her eccentricity,
perhaps because I am limited by my own perception.

If only I could soar with wings outstretched,
tips touching the bright, cold moon.

If only I could stand alone on its surface,
disposing of the unrelenting aura of my being.

If only I could see beyond the complex simplicity,
of the balance of nature and man.

If only …
        then I could be content.

She smiles as her eyes recede into a vortex of moonlight,
        distant and distant becoming,
until her final transformation into the nightingale
        is complete.

To wish and desire her innocence.

To become life's intention … Simple.

A MELODY FROM NIGHTINGALE'S NEST

what say thee, my love?
new moons transfixed in gaze,
perhaps it is within your autumn journey,
   you are blinded by a winter haze.

the tips of your fingers glance,
and dance in the rise of the sun,
petals peddle underfoot,
   your hand the chrysanthemum.

oh, heart of heart, it flutters,
beneath the fury of a gold-crowned crest,
it beats in the elation of harmony,
   to the melody from nightingale's nest.

your golden hair windswept,
tangled in the clearest, evening sun,
you walk and walk then disappear,
   horizon is night's coercion.

so what say thee, my love?
when time shall finally break,
and I take the last of my winter walks
   upon your field of keepsakes.

I will ask you to remember,
our love lived in sage and blue,
from the blossom of the flower,
   to the deep rich twilight hue.

ASHES

Only moments will remain,
in this box filled with memories.

I cannot predict which memories you will keep,
or how you will remember me.

I can only strive for my life's intention.

I know only that ashes are like songs,
sounds which disappear into the sunset horizon,
and rest only during the night.

They journey.

My ashes will be grains of sand,
scattered with the westward wind.

They will dance with the springtime flower,
and lie still within winter's blanket.

Always with a single purpose -
to journey home to your heart,

to follow you along your soul's path,
to sprinkle you with happiness,

from time to time,

until they come to finally rest
in the infinity which is you and me.

OUR GOODBYES

our goodbyes
> are drenched in teardrops,

which rise through dreams
> within infinite time-warps.

we implode then burst
> from the black soul of star hearts.

I ask only
> when my time comes,

you extinguish
> the memories of my face,

unless it is the bursting star-gleam from my eyes.

perhaps then,
> it may be best to be remembered.

EXCEPT TO YOU

And so, it must be, my love,
the final words exhumed from

the depths of my lungs, like a mummy
risen from the pyramids in Egypt.

It is the conclusion as it approaches.
It is the period after the final sentence.

It is the final note of a song.
It is the final lyric of a poem.

It is the applause,
as the curtain collapses.

It is my final sleep,
my final goodbye.

It is whispers into the wind,
and echoes drifted away.

It is unceremonious, my love,
except to you,

except to you.

ACKNOWLEDGEMENTS

Many thanks to everyone who has made this collection possible, especially those who have provided insight at some point in the creative or editing process of certain poems – Sarah Maples, J. Rogan Kelly, Taz Ruffilo, Kelly Bergin, Renee Ashley, Kathy Graber, Walter Cummins, and Eileen Janowitz.

I would like to thank my family, friends, and in-laws, all whom have been supportive of all my creative endeavors.

A huge thank you to you, the reader. By supporting me, you support the dream of all Indie Authors.

Most of all, thank you to my wife, Cory Lynn Pearson. Without you, this dream would have never come true. Every day, I look forward to where our journey will take us.

***

FOLLOW KENNETH ON SOCIAL MEDIA

Instagram: @kennethfrancispearson
Twitter: @kfpearson

Visit Kenneth's Website at:
www.kfpearson.com

***

Finally, Kenneth would love to hear your review of the book.

Kindly leave a review on Goodreads, Amazon, Barnes & Noble, Indigo, etc. or email him at kfpears@gmail.com!

CPSIA information can be obtained
at www.ICGtesting.com
Printed in the USA
LVHW010804140921
697777LV00006B/88

9 780976 854302